ROSARY MADE OF AIR

OTHER BOOKS BY JOSEPH MASSEY

Full-length:

Areas of Fog (Shearsman, 2009)
At the Point (Shearsman, 2011)
To Keep Time (Omnidawn, 2014)
Illocality (Wave, 2015)
A New Silence (Shearsman, 2019)

Chapbooks:

Minima St. (Range, 2003)
Eureka Slough (Effing Press, 2005)
Bramble (Hot Whiskey, 2005)
Property Line (Fewer & Further, 2006)
November Graph (Longhouse, 2007)
Out of Light (Kitchen Press, 2008)
Within Hours (Fault Line Press, 2008)
The Lack Of (Nasturtium Press, 2009)
Exit North (Book Thug, 2010)
Mock Orange (Longhouse, 2010)
Another Rehearsal for Morning (Longhouse, 2011)
Thaw Compass (Press Board Press, 2014)
An Interim (Tungsten Press, 2014)
What Follows (Ornithopter Press, 2015)
5 Poems (Tungsten Press, 2018)
Present Conditions (Hollyridge Press, 2018)
Backroad Scroll (Longhouse, 2019)
Unsent (Wrack Line Editions, 2019)
No Omen (Otata's Bookshelf, 2019)
On the Cusp (Tungsten Press, 2021)

ROSARY MADE OF AIR

Poems

Joseph Massey

THE EXILE PRESS

2022

Joseph Massey, *Rosary Made of Air*
First published in 2022
by The Exile Press

Typesetting & Design: Gerry Cambridge

ISBN: 9798417898099

Contents

Breath Work / 9
Portal / 19
A Way Through / 21
Winter / 22
Manifesto / 23
The Shape of Something Said / 28
Late Time / 30
Keepsake / 33
Poem Against Cancellation / 34
To a New Friend / 36
Satori in Easthampton / 37
September 8th, 2021 / 38
Backroad Scroll / 40
Altar and Offering / 49
On the Cusp / 65
The Turn / 74
The Walk / 75
Winter Solstice / 76
Year's End / 77
Removed / 78

Acknowledgements / 80

I know the shadow
is no less alive than my
hand holding it there

Breath Work

i.

Even if there were a world
it wouldn't bother to be ours.
We know the mind is better left lost

and each thing it feigns to anchor.
It's enough to just sit—
to breathe each other here,

awake in what language lacks,
while a jagged line of late gulls

vanishes into a low cloud
that says snow but doesn't.

ii.

Snow plows vibrate the walls
and the water in a vase shakes:
flowers that fail
to fool my room away from winter

sit on a speaker blaring news:
panic sapped into fatigue.
I navigate the day
through windows, shadows

barring the floor; I track the season
by what sticks to sewer grates.
Today they're under half a foot of snow.
I'm walking in it, hungover, hovering

over a notebook to chisel a phrase.
Sky's gray grain gathering white.
White enclosing white.
A clean and marginless page.

iii.

Sunday is the ritual of Sunday
repeating its name
until it disintegrates.
What remains: half-dead
grocery store flowers
losing blue petals on the altar.

And this thoughtless sense of light lengthening
despite the darkness in the room.

iv.

Memory's a husk hung to dry
in sunbeams latticed over a parking lot
snowbank. Crushed Coke can
lodged at the peak.

A shadow that would claim me
rocks on its heels by a pile of slush;
but the weather is heavier
than superstition,
and I am unburdened.

I is a witness,
mere consciousness
navigating the edge
of the cusp
of spring.

v.

After death-deep sleep
I wait for the day's first omen.

Skinned black branches
wind lashes between clouds
that make the mountain small.

The mountain still snowed over
even after last night's rain. White

creased russet with traprock. This
is the counterpoint to the wind

and what it can't articulate, this
stone holding the horizon down.

vi.

At dusk starlings roost
in the belfry of a closed
Catholic church. Wood
warped by how many winters—
too soft to throw an echo.

vii.

First few signs of spring
and mania animates

the dormant corners.
What my mind cannot contain

the field contains—the light shakes.

Clouds stacked in Robert
Lax stanzas disperse behind

the mountain—a kind
of vapor now—a blue plume

the sun pulls further apart.

viii.

Mountain made bald
by a microburst.

Ridge stubbled
with new growth

stilts the cloud veil.
I'll sit

until the last patch of snow
dissolves into stone.

ix.

Spring coming in, coming on.

March is mud
and bright dusk,
liminal and littered; a pause
before forsythia, honeysuckle,
alleys overwhelmed with weeds.

Roots breathe beneath receding snow.

x.

Cold rain claws dusk. I
close the window and listen.
The perfect poem
is without words, is the thing
itself thoughtlessly ringing.

Portal

Second day
of spring
and winter stilts
the signal: snow
in truncated gusts
performs its math
over what
the window
frames. Lines
between lawn
and sidewalk
fade; hedges
heavy, dusted,
heave into
wind, white
and whiter now,
a peripheral
blur, as I turn
in my chair
between stacks
of unread books.
Basement apartment—
grass stubble
claws at glass,
pockets
of darkness
other weather
won't reach.

Insect-pocked
soil, fast food
trash scattered
by a raccoon,
the vibration
of a passing
plow. Almost
underground,
time uncoils
without shadow's
measure, and
I leave
my clock
unplugged.
I live to see
particulars decay
and to graph them
with breath
and the sound
I send
through breath.

A Way Through

When the poem reminds you
you're breathing, alive
within a language
that leaves you
wordless, even as
grief pixelates
the hour
and this voice
that serves
as company
and compass
in December's dark
draws you toward
the margin, what
the words wash up
against, wrack zone
of sound, rubble
of sound, from which
morning emerges.
Through shallow sun
snow ambles in a spiral
narrowing into traffic—
falls and continues to fall
into its own disappearance.

Winter

under ice
a mandala
of maple leaves

Manifesto

i.

Poetry's enough
to sustain
the day.
Sliced June light
fills a crystal
vase sitting
on a sill's
cracked white
paint: emptiness
brimming over
a name, bloom-
ing into shadow.

ii.

Nothing other
than now—
than this—

white moth
navigating
honeysuckle

coiled around
a wrought iron
handrail.

iii.

Notice
the breath.
And when it

lengthens
watch the mind
unspool

into pond water
repeating
clouds.

iv.

In June's lucid dream
rain blurs a world
into focus

and the poem appears
where it always was—

before you.

v.

The sound of the pencil
writing the sound
of the rain.

The Shape of Something Said

No time beyond daylight
waving on the floor

like spilled water, and so it goes.
This window won't hold

the omens that pass. My mind
haunts my body as my body

haunts the room
and there's a glitch

in the quiet, an inked-in echo.
Sleep is a relief.

Sleep and poetry.
Not words, but the space

around words
anchors me to an hour.

Across the street
forsythia bursts from black rubble.

Even inside, I'm surrounded
by what wakes in April.

No time beyond shadows
spilled around windows.

A nameless tree's makeshift sundial
sliding deeper into the mulch.

Late Time

The weather is panic
evaporated into gusts

of cold sun. White sun
cracking gray clouds

bulked low
on the horizon.

What am I
but an animal

lumbering
through a late time

waiting for
an impossible spring,

waiting for
the mind to settle,

for static to sink
beneath song.

I wait for relief.
I wait for the heart

to open, for
the voice to thaw.

And sparrows,
how do they survive

hollow-boned
in an arctic blast?

Yesterday's news:
wet confetti

scattered over
curbside slush.

Cold, white sun
lands across my face

as I turn a corner;
and I am weightless

without a name,
nameless without

a form, dissolved
into particulars

unspooled into
consciousness,

unwinding
into a world

never more
than now.

Keepsake

The friend who betrayed
me, I hold no malice
toward him, remembering when
we drove the backroads
of Western Massachusetts,
and wild turkeys, barely lit by what red
remained of a sunset, crossed the road
and we stopped to let them pass.
We stopped talking, after hours
of talk, and watched those ghosts,
those turkey-shaped shadows,
slowly cross a narrow road
into woods where it was already night.

Poem Against Cancellation

Vow to see
what isn't
immediately
seen, what
takes time
to sift
into view;
takes time
and keeps time
as the gift
of a space
in which
to perceive
the inverse
of surface,
and to know
the world
is many—
many worlds
within.
No voice
is single—
a tapestry
of history
and pitch—
and to hear it

is to receive it
without
surrendering
to an impulse
to destroy it.
Say the un-
kempt shrub
is full of bees
and bees
weave sun
through a new
season. Say
there's no account-
ing for the world
and how it
defies
a frame. Say
within the one—
within you—
infinities
flourish.

To a New Friend

Daylight disassembles into sound—
the hum I hold in my head
is the hum you hold in your head, too.
The poem, written or unwritten,
is enough to see us through the thaw.

Soon the fields will fill with names.

Mud will rupture with indescribable color.

Satori in Easthampton

The sun crests over Family Dollar. I narrow my sight to see spring's debris drift across the parking lot. Dandelion seed heads sheathe wind. The shape of the wind; the grain of the light. Today there's joy in the blur. To seize time by saying what surrounds me, when words instantly slip from the surfaces they feign to reflect. As if language were an anchor and not a kind of scar tissue. Today there's joy in the voice that falters to locate me here.

September 8th, 2021

Poetry went cold
this summer.

The days
wouldn't translate

into a phrase.
The world

was what reached
through the weather

I was under.
My mind mirrored

a room
vibrating at night

in cricket-dense quiet.
All that's left

of summer:
a cloud deck skims

the top
off a mountain

and a sun-bleached
lottery ticket

snagged by prongs
of Russian sage

tongues
the chlorinated air.

Backroad Scroll

Frog-croak
metronome
drones from
the yard's edge:

green deepening
green; deepening
black. What calls
culls a sense

of distance—
the unseen
seen
through sound.

•

After two days
of rain
spring's

sacrificial
flower
rusts

the fields
yellow.
Yellow en-

trenched in
green deep-
ening green

under low
cloud shade.

•

Constant bird clamor
  gives the hours
depth and texture—
  an illegible net
of noise
  made legible
once the mind withdraws
  to let only light in.

•

In a cardinal's wake
a red streak

gashed clear
through gauzy haze.

•

To let only light in—
to allow the mind
to withdraw. Rain

falls from sun,
sky bright beyond
description.

•

Hay bales tied tight in a field
spaced evenly apart
like phrases
toward an unfinished sentence.

•

Night birds trill
as if to trace
an illegible net
through the dark,

to contain
what contains it—

to defy it.

•

Spring's yellow
sacrificial
flower
surrounds
scrap metal
stacked beside
a weather-bleached
shed.

•

Off-white,
off-yellow—
    both—tulip
poplar flowers
    cloud sky
    pale
    with heat.

•

Japanese rose shrub
  spilled up and over
    the back of the shed

levitates—countless
  flowers webbed—
    a singular white blur—

under the Blue
  Flower Moon's
    gray glister.

•

From this angle
low clouds lean
into scrub, dense
at the back end
of the yard. Wander
        toward the center
where a space in weeds
and branches frames
a white farmhouse,
white fence,
        silver silo
        propping up
        half-sunk sun.

when the rain reminds you
you're alive
before it begins to fall

Altar and Offering

i.

Through November's
arterial horizon
traffic flickers.
Mountain bare

but for a bent cloud
clipping the ridge.
What would it mean
to see clearly—

to know
nothing's there
other than what is.

ii.

A clearing
between scrub
and birches peeling

(white sheets flagging)
where sunset sparks.

And those hollow tones:
geese gathered at the river's
gravel bank.

They're not singing;
they're sounding out

a sequence of notes
describing the color
and shape of the cold.

iii.

The poem begins without a word
while I walk through sideways snow.

Snow barbed by a gone season.

There's joy in the unsaid and how it accumulates.

This god-vacant pain, the run-on days, disrupted.

iv.

The day before
the longest night

of the year,
December sun

snags runoff
from last week's

snowfall—
a silver cord binding

my eyes to asphalt,
traffic, dead leaf

floating in the flash.
Overnight rain

rearranged
the mountain:

white to red,
faint red

pulse
under russet.

Blinded again,
I'm rooted

to a world
without me.

Wordless prayer
—this vacancy

where the new life begins.

v.

Streetlight
suspends hail
in a sepia orb.

The fricative hiss
as stripped trees
sift it. I hear it

as language
refusing
to become speech.

A circular breath
extinguishing
the familiar.

vi.

Open the blinds
to snowlight—
that bright, particular pain.

There, in the shock,
locate the real

before it sinks
into synesthesia.

This is how winter
makes itself useful:

it tricks the body

to trick
the mind still.

vii.

Up late listening
to rain run ice

into mud.
Does the room
contain sound

or does sound
contain the room?

Walls dissolve
in the dark—
a locked door opens.

viii.

I covet the cold,

how it punctures
memory

and dislodges
the rot. When

wind
is enough—

harsh enough—
to smother thought.

ix.

Clouded
by snow fog

a snowed-over
mountain—mind

makes it
visible.

x.

After the snow squall
sun mutes
what snow remains
in my vision, and the figure

on the other side of the crosswalk

too bright to say

walking toward
or away from me.

xi.

A few days lost
to a false spring.
Black slush caged
by bolts of light.

My mind, jolted,
turned jagged;
but last night
the cold returned

and when I woke
morning was a window
in the shape of a field
draped in frozen fog.

xii.

A vulture circles
a shotgun's echo, carving

into cloudless sky
the shape of the field below.

The air alone
both altar and offering.

before the next breath
pause, and find
the poetry there

On the Cusp

i.

Time condenses
beyond me; the lines
hold a whole season.
Signs by which to see
when false weather
blurs the real. How
this God-quiet husk—
what waits to be said—
lights the dark
swarming toward us.

ii.

Underground, I trace
the changing season
by texture alone. Beams
of sidelong sun cut
through a thin slit of glass;
they brace the floor
beneath me
and move slowly
to hold the table to my hand.

iii.

The way the light grows
viscous, gold
around the edges.
This hazy levitation of grief.
To begin again—
anointed by Your silence—
when August was all I thought I knew.

iv.

Alive, finally, in the afterlife
of summer, I walk home
in the gloaming, and the mind
stops chiming. When panic
exhausts itself the colors
return, the world returns:
Orange bending into red, yellow
blending into lavender sweeping
the horizon, punctured by white
headlights. The gift is given. I walk
and watch my hand rock
in its own shadow like a bell.

v.

As the days narrow
and shadows lengthen, burrow
in words that cast light
before night consumes the room
and dead leaves rattle windows.

vi.

Outside of the window
snow devils rise
and unwind
in horizontal snowfall.
I read the glass, a wordless
book. Wordless, but full of
phrases—motion and texture.
An outline of silence
filled in by silence.

vii.

I walk to channel an hour
away from pain,
face in full-blasted sun.
January sun—sudden, startles
the mind quiet. Swallows lift off
all at once from the power line
and the sound is singular, a gasp,
a sheet of thick paper torn fast.

viii.

I wander through
the shell called winter.
Hollow wreck of stripped limbs
where the sun, small now, droops.
Mindless blessing—
the gift of consciousness.
I'm stranded in a body
that barrels beyond me,
splayed white rays
distorting my vision.

ix.

To navigate pain
with language alone.
The language of the dead
cuts a moment close
and time collapses.
I'm alive in the company.
"Urge and urge and urge…"
The heart settles, held
by breath breaking
into sound, my body
merging into words.

The Turn

Awake in the pre-dawn dark
at the end of a difficult year,

I gather scraps from a notebook
to contain grief
in private speech.

The words repeat like a rosary:

sun, silence, time,
light, day, pain.

As if ink could snare a voice
beyond me—for company—

and dissolve the "I"
in an image
at once blurred and vivid.

That was the vow and the dream.

Morning, bright now
between the margins—

cloud, window,
sparrow, rain—

at the end of a difficult year.

The Walk

At dusk, the lamps
flick on behind windows—

that spectral,
amber glow—
and I'm dizzy

with nostalgia
for an almost forgotten dream.

At dusk, shadows deepen

before they fade,
engraved

in asphalt
and old snow
slumped like ash against a curb.

I hold my hands to my face
and breathe into my palms:
Thank God.

Thank God
for the freezing wind—

my mind stops.

Winter Solstice

White sun quartered
by pine limbs.
The wind stings.
Gravestones loose long
shadows over the path.
I walk in the margins;
I read the names.
To go on talking to myself
for warmth and company
while gulls chant
the blank sky full—
and the line breaks
behind a bruised horizon.

Year's End

What began with bewilderment
ends with fatigue. Pixelated
days dispersed into static
we mistook for speech.
We stopped listening
how many shocks ago.
The horror and how it hollows.
One way out
is to locate grace in a walk
and receive a tree's bare
but bright frequency.
Notice the waxing gibbous
afternoon moon
smudged above a shuttered
Bank of America—lucent,
resigned to its transparency.
See starlings
expand and collapse
like lungs exhaling dusk.
Now the long night,
a long silence
if we'll let it find us.

Removed

Another faceless
season. Eyes pass
narrowed by fear

and hollow
in the lull
of language
lost
to hell.

To survive:
marvel
at the unraveling
of a world
that was never
yours.

Wake early.

Allow
the soundless hours
to wash over

and become
the poem.

Is it life if it
isn't death—
the cycle of breath—

the silent
prayer your body
becomes—this

poem between us.

Acknowledgements

Thanks to Wolfram Swets who published many of these poems as broadsides and chapbooks over the last several years under his Tungsten Press imprint. Thanks to *Dreamstreets, Tablet, Longhouse, Trinity House,* and every other magazine and journal who first published these poems.

Glory be to God.

Made in the USA
Middletown, DE
16 April 2022